S0-BNJ-253

Footsteps Beside Him

by
Nettie Hall

HALL'S SLEDS
Jeanette (Nettie) Hall
2143 Robinson Road, Apt.3
Jackson, Michigan 49203
(517)768-1139
E-Mail: Hallssled@juno.com

©2011 Jeanette (Nettie) Hall. All rights reserved.

No part of this book may be reproduced, stored in a retrieval system, or transmitted by any means without the written permission of the author.

First Published by Halls Sleds 3/01/2011

ISBN: 978-0-615-43817-7

Printed in the United States of America
Chelsea, Michigan

This book is printed on acid-free paper.

Preface by Margaret Harvey-
She is the gal who makes sled dog racing go in Michigan. She is president of GLSDA, liaison officer for MUSH and GLSDA, and treasurer and regional director of region 6 for ISDRA. She is the best timer in the sled dog world (my opinion) and my good friend.

Acknowledgements:
Thank you to all the dog sledders that made my adventures possible and made Hall's Sleds a fun business.
I would also like to thank Margaret Harvey for selling my book for me, Carole Straayer for being my dear friend and Carrie Hair for helping self publish this book.

Contents

Preface...*vii*

GETTING STARTED...*1*

SOME OTHER EXPERIENCES ON THE TRAILS.................*7*

SOME OF MY DEAREST LEAD DOGS............................*21*

SOME OF MY YOUNG KENNEL HELPERS
OR DRIVERS..*41*

ON BEING PRESIDENT OR
SOMETHING ON THE GLSDA BOARD............................*51*

RETIRING FROM RACING IN THE MIDDLE YEARS.......*55*

HUNTING..*61*

BUILDING OUR HOUSE AND CABIN..............................*63*

TEACHING...*73*

BACK ON THE FARM...*75*

MY FINAL YEARS...*83*

Preface

I can't honestly tell you the exact moment I met Nettie Hall. I don't remember what day it was, what year it was or where we were at the moment of our first encounter. I only remember how comfortable I felt being with Nettie and getting to know her, how much I have enjoyed her company each and every time we were together from that moment on and how I have always admired her unpretentious and unassuming personality. Knowing Nettie means getting to know yourself even better as she seems to bring out the best in everyone she encounters. Knowing Nettie means to sled dog enthusiasts that you are in the company of one of the greats, not necessarily a person who has won every event she has entered, but one who has been a leader in the evolution of the sport of dog sledding in the Great Lakes area to what it is today, by being a patient mentor to newcomers and being a good ambassador for the sport overall. Nettie has always been a strong advocate for good dog care, safe trails and the involvement of the whole family. She has a passion and conviction for the sport that has always been evident through her unparalleled participation. My husband, Rick, and I have a gavel in our possession, a gavel on which are engraved the names of everyone who has been President of the Great Lakes Sled Dog Association since the time the group was formed and records were kept. On this gavel the name Nettie Hall appears, not once, twice, or three times, but 11 times since 1959. That is true dedication, in my eyes . . . dedication to an organization, to a sport and to a membership who she has guided with her knowledge and experience, her wisdom and expertise.

I have been with Nettie during good times and also some not so good times. I was with Nettie in the Upper Peninsula of Michigan the day that Frank's sled-building workshop burned. I was with her many times during Frank's long illness, his death and the difficult days and weeks afterward. But I was also with Nettie in June of 2000 when I was blessed with the opportunity to present her with a well- deserved honorary membership into the International Sled Dog Racing Association. Our family also was fortunate to be able to be in her company at sled dog races for many years, traveling around Michigan as well as other states. I recall Nettie's excitement as we traveled back from a race in Wisconsin across the U.P. during the middle of the night, and as we passed a casino she sat bolt upright hoping we would stop. "Sorry Nettie, we just want to get home!" On more than one occasion, I have seen Nettie on a mission fighting for a cause she believes in, which she will grip like the jaws of a pit bull until she achieves the outcome she is looking for.

I can only imagine how students of Nettie's must have felt all those years she spent teaching. I hope they realize how lucky they were to have such a great woman for their teacher. Her patience and gentle ways had to have molded many kids into fine young men and women during the years of her teaching career.

Spending afternoons at the Hall residence in Jackson were the highlights of many of our days. Whether Frank and Nettie were working together in the shop building sleds, working in the kennel with the dogs or just sitting around their kitchen table talking, you knew you were welcome and knew they considered you a friend after you left. Frank took our youngest son, Ryan, out into the 'back 40' one afternoon and let him target practice with one of his guns. Ryan still has that target to this day, knowing what it meant to have Frank take you out shooting.

It is difficult to express what a daunting task I faced when I was asked to try to put into a short page or two all of the things I have seen and felt over the years that I have known this remarkable woman. Hopefully in the pages that follow, you will get a glimpse into the life and loves of Nettie Hall, my friend, my 'other mom', a woman whom many have affectionately dubbed "Grandma Nettie". Enjoy!

Margaret Harvey

GETTING STARTED

I'll <u>NEVER</u> forget my first sled dog race! I had graduated from college and was teaching in Grandville, Michigan. Frank, my husband (acquaintance at that time), took me to see what this strange sport was all about!

I went armed with a still camera and a super eight movie camera. Frank was on the loud speaker. I ran from the starting line to the finish line to Frank to starting line, etc. I had never seen either a husky or a malamute (typical sled dogs at that time). They were beautiful and so full of enthusiasm and joy that one could not help but be excited with them. I had never been so enthralled in my life.

A year later, he took me to a race in Roscommon, Michigan. There was Jerry with a three month old puppy. She was absolutely adorable. Frank bought it for my birthday—which is in the summer but I got it in around February. We called her Silver. She was my first lead dog.

I need to tell you about my first race. It was probably another year later.

We had four dogs. I got to use three of them. I left the one female out because the two girls hated each other and let me tell you that you have never experienced a dog fight until you have two female malamutes trying to kill each other. Frank ran in the men's race. Then I used the same dogs in the women's race. The trail was an oval around 2-3 miles long. We were just going along and I got so tired, I had to sit in my sled for a minute to catch my breath. Joann came along and passed me. She asked if I was ok. I said I just had to rest a minute. She looked at me rather strangely as she flew by. I finished the race but I guess I was the joke of the day!

Later that year Frank ran four dogs in a 25 mile race. He went from Petoskey to Harbor Springs and back. The second day (races are usually 2 day affairs running the same trail both days). Umiak (his strongest dog) developed a urine infection (blood in his urine) and he had to drop him (not run him). He thought he should probably scratch but being the loving wife as I was, I told him he shouldn't be chicken. When he finished, he said he'd never been so tired in his life. I really felt a little bad about it then.

One of the results of that race was that Frank resolved that we would never be short of dogs again. He set to work that week making a new dog carrier (individual boxes to carry the dogs on their way to and from races). He made it to hold 10 dogs. At the time we had purchased a lead dog, Smoky, so that made five dogs. His competitors thought he had picked up a bunch of dogs that week and were concerned about how big his team was going to be that weekend. He just ran five dogs.

The next year we did have enough dogs. We had had a litter of pups. One of the great lessons I learned as a kennel owner—puppies grow up to be dogs! This can be a lot of problems for a beginning—or older—dog driver because 6 puppies can almost be held in your arms but 6 dogs each need a chain or pen in your kennel. Besides many townships have a limit or charge more for more dogs. Anyway, in the fall we trained all the dogs and puppies.

Frank ran in the men's class. I did a little trick in the women's class. I used his same lead dogs but added a couple fresh dogs to my team. My competitor's ran the same dogs as their husband. That year I ran seven races and won every one of them.

In one race near the end of the season, I overheard Ruth talking to her lead dog, Boots. Her husband had bought her from New England earlier in the year but she hadn't dared run Boots yet. She didn't see me but was telling Boots how important it was to beat me that day. I was sure she was going to do so because I was using sweet old malamute, Silver, who was steady but not really what you'd call speedy. I came in first and found that Ruth's team had come in before me but no Ruth. To win, all the dogs in the team and the driver need to cross the finish line. Boots took a corner too fast for Ruth. She was thrown off the sled and hit her head on a tree which I think knocked her out. They had to go out and get her. Silver and I talked about it and felt real sorry for her. Ruth never raced again!!!

After several years of racing women's class, Class B, 5 dog class, and 7 dog class, I decided I was ready for unlimited. I helped Frank get his No. 1 team trained. Then we trained my No. 2 team. I prepared a 9 dog team as compared to Frank's 14 dog team. The Grand Rapids Press ran a big article about this woman who was going to challenge the men in the unlimited class. There were 4 teams of the same caliber as Frank's team and any one of them could win. I figured I could take 5th place if I didn't make too many mistakes.

Mistake number one came the week before the race. As I was training my team, I got my finger caught in the gangline. When I finally got the mess untangled, I had a very sore finger. I spent the rest of the week teaching with a bandage around the finger, trying to write on the board. I finally went to the family doctor after school on Friday. He sent me to the bone specialist and he said I needed to have an operation the next day or I'd have a stiff finger the rest of my life. I said I couldn't do that because I needed to race in a race the next day. It was so advertised I just couldn't let my public down. He said it was my choice!

I ran the race with my 2 fingers taped together so they wouldn't hurt so much. I took off and was very careful that I made no mistakes on the trail. The amazing thing was that I immediately found you just can't run a team with 2 fingers bound together so I took the bandage off and it didn't hurt me a bit. When I came in, I nearly passed out because it hurt so much. That just shows you what adrenaline can do for you! I knew there were some problems when along the trail I passed Frank tied up to a tree fixing some problem in his team. (This is not good for the number 2 team to pass the number 1 team from the same kennel). When I had rebandaged my fingers and the times came in, I ended up in 1st place. Evidently the other 3 had had problems of some kind too. It is very easy to have problems while running 11-14 dogs. The second day I went out first and the final score put me in 2nd place. If you see a bunch of kkk's in my typing, you'll recognize that I never did get that finger fixed.

That year the guys all knew that if they had problems, that darn Nettie was going to beat them. I didn't have the fastest team but I had pretty much a trouble free team which was true during most of my races. They voted for Driver of Year trophy for that year and I won it. Tom really felt he deserved it and I sort of think he did. But more people voted for me so there you are!!

At one time we had 75 dogs in our kennel. This is when Mike Murfin came from Minnesota to learn how to run a team of dogs. We had his dogs plus two unlimited teams for us, a seven dog team for Dean and a 3 dog team for Rick. We had lots of help so it didn't seem like too much work. We urged each other on so it made all our teams better. One fall training session we went with 42 dogs. Although training sessions were for training, we still had them timed. This was practice for the timers and also helped us to judge our teams against our competition.

Frank took first in the unlimited; I took a fourth. Mike took first in the 7 dog; Dean took second. Rick took first in 3 dog. We were not popular as we left the training session but we were a jolly group with high expectations for the year.

Frank and I got married on April 12, 1962.
We lived in a house trailer at first

Nettie Hall

Some Other Experiences on the Trails

In the early years, we decided to have a race in Jackson, our hometown. We convinced Frank's boss to put $500 into the race for prizes. This was the first time we had a purse. I'm not sure this was good because when there is money involved, it seems like some of the fun goes away. Well, it didn't in this race. We snowshoed a trail around Ella Sharp Park. It was about 2 miles long. It seemed very long when we made it, but the first team made it in about 5 minutes so it couldn't be very long.

The day of the race, Jackson Citizen Patriot came out with a full page story of our kennel and our training trails. I think they were about a mile long also. Anyway, many people in Jackson decided this would be a great way to spend a Sunday afternoon!! We had one huge traffic jam. Many of my friends and students at school said they spent the day on the road and when they got to the park, the action was all over. The neat thing was that Frank and I each took 1st place trophies which I still have. I guess I learned a lot about organization that day.

One of the races in the unlimited class took us out in the countryside, past a monastery on a road where you were to turn left to continue on the trail. We were scooting right along and when we came to the left turn I gave Boots a very firm Gee (right turn please) and of course Boots couldn't read trail signs too well and had never been on the trail before so she obediently turned right. I went flying by the monastery where the monks were just getting out and about. Imagine their surprise to see a 9 dog team go by. I waved merrily to them, found a trail (probably an old snowmobile trail) that lead me back to the road, and got back on the trail. When I came to that left hand turn I gave a very firm Hah and believe it or not, Boots took the hah without a hesitation. It is most common for a lead dog to want to follow the trail they had run before. I'll always remember the shocked look on the face of those monks.

We were racing in Lake City. The former owners of

Nanook came down from Ranger Lake to see their little dog compete. We started near the shore of the lake and went off the lake, over the humped shore and soon after went straight ahead avoiding a right hand turn that took us along the shore. I left before Frank so in this situation, he needed to go to the starting line and leave without his main helper's assistance. It was rather a hard trail because a lot of it was on roads and the roads were barely snow covered which made it hard to stop or make corrections. When I got back home (to the finish line) I looked up and saw Nanook visiting in the car with his past owners. He seemed real happy but Frank didn't appear too elated. He had taken the right turn down the shore road where he could no way stop a 13 dog team and ended up coming to the lake by a back way.

We were racing on the sand dunes near Saugatuck. I was running an unlimited team with 11 dogs in it. We had purchased a puppy called Randy—after his daddy the famous Bryar dog called Brandy. This was his first race. As we approached one down hill, a trail help person yelled, "Watch the hill coming up!!"

I didn't hear him so turned around and asked, "What?!!" By then my team was hurdling down a steep hill with a frozen clod in the middle. I hit it sideways which not only threw me off my sled but caught the sled in such a way that it broke both uprights on one side. These hold the sled bed to the runners. Luckily the trail help placed at the bottom of that hill was an expert trail helper. Whenever I saw Tom E. along the trail I had no problem letting him hold my sled while I fixed my problem. As a matter of fact, I often waited until I got to him to fix things.

Tom caught my team. I ran down the hill to get back on the sled. It immediately became known to both of us that Randy had decided this running in a sled dog team was not for him. We loaded him on the sled. Now we have a dog bag on our sled to put a dog into when we load him but we did not at that time. I just snapped him into the sled and went on my way. We soon turned onto the Lake Michigan shoreline and followed that for some time. There were chunks of ice all along and in the trail. My sled was broken in such a way that the uprights would slip off the runners and I had to lift them on as I went down the trail. The only thing holding the sled together was the rawhide ties Frank had used to tie the uprights to the runners. So there I went—dodge the ice chunks, hold Randy on the sled, put the uprights back on the runners, dodge the ice chunks, grab Randy as he tried to escape, fix the sled, etc, etc, etc. I made it in. I worked on Randy all that summer and he definitely overcame his problem. He became Frank's dog just behind lead in the best team he ever drove.

Randy when he was grown and Frank's point dog

Another race I remember is when I was running a six dog

team in Ely, Minnesota. Frank ran in the unlimited and I competed in the 6 dog class. Against me were real great mushers from California, Michigan, Minnesota, and Ohio. One, Judy, was a gal that most thought would win the race hands down. There was a driver from California who was not well known to me anyhow. We raced in duel starts (two teams started at the same time). The tricky part of this is that the one hasn't really caught the other team and therefore might not have to right to ask them to stop their team and let her pass. You can ask them this if you gained a minute or so on them. I did finally leave my pair mate in the dust and caught Judy. She did not want to let me pass (which of course I had the right to ask her) and told me that I had caught her and therefore should be satisfied since I had obviously beat her. I kept telling her there was another driver ahead of us that I needed to catch. She finally let me by or rather I guess she had a slight problem and I went by and left her in my dust. I drove like a raving maniac to pick up time on the guy ahead of me. He beat me by 2 seconds!! Judy went around complaining about my poor sportsmanship which really made me angry because just the year before I had won the top sportsmanship award from our local racing association.

One of the times I was president of GLSDA (Great Lakes Sled Dog Association), I got myself in a real mess! I got this brilliant idea that we should have, along with Championship trophies and Driver of the Year trophies, a trophy for lead dog of the year. It wasn't long before the whole club realized what a problem I had. Of course, Frank thought that our lead dog, Nanook, should be the obvious choice. As a matter of fact, he thought that if I chose another dog, he might make life very difficult for me! Use your complete imagination! Tom was equally sure that since he was beating Frank that year that his lead dog would be the definite choice. I even thought my Millie should be given a thought! As the year neared its end and the annual meeting was coming up—we always gave awards at that time, I began to perspire and the whole club was holding its breath and discussing what I was going to do to get out of this mess. When the time came I presented the trophy with this speech:

On Presenting Lead Dog of the Year Trophy

Let me start by saying that any dog who can lead a large dog team over a long race trail and complete it as marked—passing teams (head on or otherwise) and being passed, making choices at corners, setting a pace that the dogs can sustain, keeping the line taut, and always listening to the driver's command—this is a great dog! To his driver, he is the best lead dog of the year.

We choose a driver of the year and if we are not chosen, we only say, "He is a good driver!"

We have a championship trophy and if we don't win it, we say, "Well, he was more consistent even if I do have a better team."

But when it comes to choosing a lead dog of the year, one becomes rather prejudiced. No matter what anyone says, he knows that he has the best lead dog. He may not be winning because he just doesn't have the dogs behind him. He may make mistakes but they all do sometimes. He's been out on the trail with his lead dog 20-40-60 or more feet ahead of him leading his team. He has made beautiful decisions on corners. Others don't know about these things but he does!!

There is a relationship between a man and his lead dog that is beyond explanation. There is a fierce loyalty between a man and his lead dog. You can condemn him but don't condemn his lead dog.

Considering this, I have put 9 names on the trophy – each one a regular Class A lead dog. It reads as follows:

In Memory of Lead Dog, "Boots"

LEAD DOG OF THE YEAR

Nanook Troubles Blaze
Minto Whitey Spunk
Frosty Tippy Millie

And all other dogs able to lead a
good sized team, past, present, future

Last meeting I said I hoped we loved our dogs enough that we could overcome prejudice and make a fair decision. Now I realize that that we can't make a fair decision for just the opposite reason – We love our dogs too much.

It's sort of like choosing the best mother. No matter what anyone says, in my heart my mother is the best mother. In my heart, my lead dog is the best lead dog.

Well, when I finished my presentation, there was barely a dry eye in the group. I think it hit them particularly hard because they were sure I was getting myself in a heap of trouble and therefore allowed themselves to be overwhelmed. They were so impressed that they insisted I read my presentation in a couple weeks to the group gathering for ISDRA (International Sled Dog Racing Association). There were a lot of damp tears in that group also.

Let me explain why you'd use a double lead instead of the typical single lead. You put your tried and true lead dog up there along with a young, fast dog. The old lead dog takes all the turns, passes or is passed by other teams and the young dog gives you speed—and learns to be a lead. Now this only works if the young goes where the old dog goes. If he pulls toward a trail that he finds interesting and the old one can't pull him over, all kinds of interesting things happen. You probably need to turn the team around and go back to the right trail. You do have to follow the trail as marked. You might set your snowhook (a hook on your sled that is put around something or in the snow to hold your team while you fix things in the team). You could try putting it in the snow but if the snow is not of the right consistency, it won't hold--especially if the team starts pulling to go. You might put it around a small tree but it better be alive or the team will yank it down. You could put it on someone's mail box pole if it is strong enough. Of course, the tree or pole needs to be near enough to the trail so you can reach it without letting go of your sled. Trail help are only on the given trail so you are left to solve your problem alone.

I usually ran a double lead because it always seemed I was training a new lead dog and this is the best or easiest way to do it.

One Christmas vacation we decided to train up north at Ranger Lake in Ontario. This was before Nanook came to live with us so we were visiting him, his owners/keepers, and Vinnie and Jeannie Canout. We had just bought a lead dog from Alaska. He came the day before we headed north. I was so excited, I left school in a hurry and jammed the car into reverse. It tore out the transmission! I guess we had it pulled to the garage but didn't let it hamper our trip. We went to the airport and picked up North (dog's name).

We loaded up our truck and dog carrier with our needs for the week, about 16 dogs, and several Hall Sleds!! On our way up Ranger Lake Rd., we got stuck. We had to put on the chains.

We had two teams--ten for Frank and six for me. Our plan was to mush from mile 19 in to Ranger Lake—mile 29 and stay overnight. The next day we would mush back the other way. We had Christmas dinner with the Canouts, mile 19. The next day we hooked up our teams. Jeannie followed with her team and rode a toboggan. That is the way she worked her dogs while trapping. Our friend, Jim, had left a couple hours earlier with one of the first snowmobiles. It had an 8 inch track. He was to pack the snow ahead of us. We weren't knowledgeable enough to know that packing just ahead of us did no good for packing-just laying a trail. We didn't need a trail because Ranger Lake Rd. was enclosed with pines weighed down with snow. There was around 2-3 foot of snow on the level.

We started out down Ranger Lake Rd. We immediately found out we had no base on our trail. The teams slogged through the snow at barely a walk. Every little bit, the teams needed to rest along with their drivers. Jeannie had no problem. She was in her element!! We found out later that she was betting that we wouldn't make it halfway before we gave up.

About 6 miles down the trail, we met Jim walking toward us. He had run out of gas. The deep snow took much more gas than we had figured. We repacked the sleds to put the gas can and Jim on Frank's sled. My team and I were so exhausted that we could not keep up. Dinner was on Jeannie's toboggan. She was going to cook dinner at Ranger Lake when we got there. While she was doing that, we were going to stake out our dogs and feed them. Obviously, we were a little delayed. I remember going by a little water fall about 3 miles before Ranger Lake. I was so thirsty that I wanted to pull my sled off to the right and get a drink but I was so exhausted that I could do nothing but hang on to my sled.

We finally got to Ranger Lake. Jeannie and Vinnie had gone ahead and had started getting things around. Vinnie had dug through the top layer of snow or ice and dipped out some water that was not from the lake but a layer up. I forget the name they had for it but Jeannie informed us that we must not drink very much of it or we would get diarrhea and sick to our stomach. We were so thirsty that every time she turned her back, we would guzzle some more water. We actually didn't get sick.

We were lucky. We had fried chicken and all the goodies. Like I said, Jeannie was in her element. She trapped in these conditions all winter.

The next day we hooked up our team. The trail was now hardened up and we flew home. We went by that waterfall not more than 100 yds. from Ranger Lake. I could not believe it. We made it back in record time. We decided to change our training plans. We went out the road a bit, turned around, and came back. Every night we stayed in Jeannie and Vinnie's log cabin.

Frank had talked about maybe building a log cabin some day. I wasn't too excited about the idea but after spending the week in their cabin, I was sold. They didn't have good insulation on the roof so there were huge ice cycles hanging to the ground. This, along with all the snow, made it a beautiful scene. Inside the log cabin, it was absolutely comfortable. It was cozy and very relaxing. We had a wonderful week. We decided we would build a log cabin and Vinnie would come and help us get started.

One of the races that I remember was the one in Mio, MI. It was not one of the earliest races because it wasn't daddy, mommy, kids but Class A, Class B, Class C, Juniors, and Kiddies. For some reason, Frank wasn't feeling too well. I think he celebrated too hard the night before. I had to drive his team in Class A and turn around and drive my team in Class B. I won both classes. Now the problem came up. No one had ever driven a team in both classes. Now days, you can race in about any class your age allows you to race. The question was should a person be allowed to run in two classes and could a person win a trophy in two classes—especially two firsts. It was to be a major debate in our association meetings for some years. Since there was no rule in place, I was given both trophies. Many contestants were not happy about it.

One of our favorite training places was five corners near Kalkaska. This was when we carried a couple snowmobiles along with our dogs and sleds. We'd use the snowmobile to check the trail—to make sure no trees were across the trail or whatever. Then after a team took off down the trail, we'd follow and pass the team in order to get to a decision place and act as trail help at that point. The snowmobile driver had to take off at top speed in order to catch the team which was no small task. Teams take off at top speed and do not slow down on curves. Snowmobiles usually need to slow down. If you were to catch the team, you couldn't slow down. This presented a problem for the rider along with me on the snowmobile.

There and at the races or other training places, I was known as hot rod Nettie. Many times I left my rider in the snow behind me. Sometimes I didn't miss them until we got to the corner we needed to get to. I'd chat along to them as we flew along. I probably wondered why they didn't answer.

Many people refused to ride with me. I was good at getting trail help out to where they belonged. I might have 3 or 4 people along with me so it was really important to get them where they belonged in a timely fashion. Sometimes the first team almost caught me so I'd tell them to hold on and give the machine a little more gas!!

One of the times we trained at five corners, Tim, Frank's good friend, came along to experience dog mushing. Although he was quite well off, he had never ridden a snowmobile before. He was a little hesitant when I gave him the keys to the machine and told him to get going. I was very surprised when he fell over on the machine just going along straight. He soon learned how to not only drive a machine but also a team of dogs. He ran a team for us that year. He had gone to Michigan State to become an expert on trees and forests. We'd pick him up as we went north through Lansing.

In one race in Mackinaw City, one of GLSDA's big races, Tim left the starting chute at the same time as I did (We had duel starts here). He beat me out of the chute and I never did make it past him until at the finish line his team decided to visit something off to the side while my team ran straight home.

One summer near the end of my mushing days, I got a call from Linda who was looking for a place to keep her dogs while she went to Michigan State to work on her Medical Degree. I imagine I told her she could keep them at my place but couldn't find a place she could rent to keep her dogs nearer Lansing. She finally decided to leave her dogs in New Mexico with her husband but she spent some time coming out to our kennel to give her a break from her stress. Many of the people training to be doctors were of a group who thought women did not belong in places of leadership or learning to be a doctor. They made life almost unbearable for her.

Linda and Armando up in Fairbanks, Alaska Their home was way up in the beautiful mountains

She used to come out in her doctor's clothes and join me in my little fenced in area and we'd lie on the ground enjoying the 4-5 week old pups. Nothing can relieve stress like a family of puppies! She'd share her problems if she wanted and I'd share my little kids. She eventually bought 4 of them and took them back to New Mexico. She went back also. Life was a lot easier in the university she went to down there. Now she is a doctor in Alaska, lives up in the mountains near Fairbanks, enjoys life, and is one of the best doctors around.

One of Frank's birthdays I thought I had a brilliant idea of what to give him. Since he usually bought what he wanted, it was very hard to buy gifts for him. One of the problems before snowmobiles or quads was how to get out on the trail to check on the driver and the team as they were training. I bought him a Honda 50. It was like a little kid's motor bike. When Frank looked in the back of the truck to see his birthday present, he got a shocked look on his face. He thought I'd really lost it. Actually, it turned out to be one of the most helpful gifts I'd ever given him. Naturally, I used it as much as or more then he did!! We'd take it along to training sessions and both of us

Checking the Trail

would get on the bike and check out the trail or whatever needed to be done.

In one of the races we had quite a bit of the trail on a road. This makes it hard to stop and fix the team with any problems that may arise. The first problem I had was with Betsy. She was a great dog but would only run on the right side. If she happened to end up on the left side, she would actually pull back and be sort of dragged. In the excitement of the start, the partner dogs got carried away and jumped over Betsy so I left the chute with her on the wrong side. Being on a road, I couldn't do anything about it until I came to the first trail help.

We were going along nicely, passing teams and going by people's driveways. They stuck right to the road until we came to this one driveway which tempted them too much. We turned in. We went up to the side of the house and on by into the deep snow. They were a strong team so this seemed like fun to them. I was getting tired so having to stop the team, go through deep snow to the lead dogs, and turn them away became almost impossible for me to do. We came up to an antique wagon out in the back yard. I thought a bit—one does not want to destroy someone's pet antique. Nothing else came in sight to help me so I took out my snowhook and hooked on the wagon. Thank goodness it held. I turned the team around, went out the driveway, and turned right to continue the race. I had to pass back many of the teams who had caught me. They wondered where I came from since I had already passed them long ago. We finished the race but I was no way near the winner. At least I did get home—which is a miracle sometimes.

At a race in North Bay, Ontario, Canada, Frank and I both raced in the open class. The French Canadians sometimes partied a little hard—as did all the mushers. I was driving down a nice, even plowed road and came upon a driver who seemed to be having an awful hard time staying on his runners. He kept falling off, dragging a ways, and then getting himself up again.

I began to worry that he might be having a health problem because the trail was so even and beautiful, he couldn't possibly be having trouble staying on his runners. When I passed him, I asked if he was OK. He said he was. I found out later that he had left the starting chute so drunk he could hardly stand up. He hadn't improved along the trail. I wonder what happened when he came to a more challenging part of the trail.

When we had quite a few dogs, we also had a pretty good dog food business going. Eagle Dog Food made a special dog food for us and we could sell it cheaply despite the fact it had 26% protein and 12% fat. Many of the coon dog hunters would stop by all times of the night and pick up their dog food needs.

I remember going to the basement, putting up the garage door, and helping many nondescript dog men without a thought that this might be dangerous. The other thing about this is we would have 6 tons of dog food in 50 lb. bags delivered at 6 A.M. This meant I could help unload all this dog food before going to school in the morning.

Some of My Dearest Lead Dogs

Silver was my first lead dog. She wasn't very fast because she was a full blooded malamute and they are like a work horse as compared to the Siberians or Alaskan dogs being race horses. She was my true friend and listened to me real good (unless there was another female around). She was my pet after she was finished racing. It is always hard to give up a good old dependable lead dog but if you wanted to win, you need to replace the good old lead dog. I needed to retire Silver.

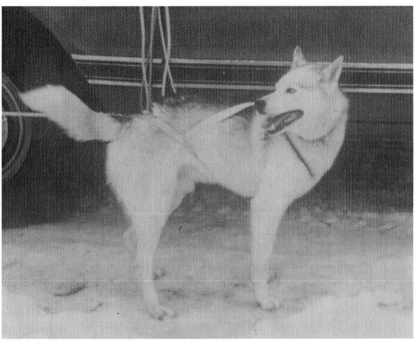

Nanook.
This picture was taken at the end of
a 25 mile per day race.
Notice that he is smiling; his line is still taught.
He was a happy dog. He knew he'd done a good job.

Nanook came from the Ranger Lake Rd. in Canada. Frank and his friend Jim bought a litter of pups and split the litter. We got three and Jim got Nanook and gave him to a friend on Ranger Lake Rd. where he would chase a Jeep down the road 10 miles to a friend, Jeannie, who had a team of dogs. Jim finally decided that Nanook was too fast to not use him in racing so we got him. He was very good as a youngun but he needed some training. Tom was a very good trainer so we sent Nanook for Frank and Chief for me over to have them trained. After they came back, I spent a whole summer working with those two dogs and they became excellent gee and haw dogs. Nanook was around 40 lbs. and Chief was about 65 lbs. What amazed me was that Nanook was stronger than Chief. He was a pure malamute while Nanook was a registered Siberian. The time I spent with Nanook was well worth it. Frank said that at one turn on the Kalkaska trail, Nanook took a turn in mid-air. That is good!

Now Chief was a different story. He was perfect on gee and haw but when I ran him in lead of my 5 dog team, I had 5 dogs running abreast. He was too slow for my other dogs. I never made that mistake again. Anyhow, I sold him to a malamute man in Cleveland, Ohio, and he was the happiest man in the state!

I put Frosty in lead. He didn't know anything but run and he stayed in the front of my team (very important). I did have a problem with Frosty though it was not his fault. We were racing along the shore of Lake Michigan up by Petosky. We ran into a patch of small stones. I fell and lost my team (I fell off the sled and they left me to run to catch up). I thought, "No problem! There always trail help at the corners. They'll catch my team. I'll run and catch up and go on with my team."

My team ad decided a right hand turn would be neat. It wasn't long and I noticed this police guy standing up by US31 with dogs all around him and with this frightened look on his face. I quickly realized my team had made a wrong turn. I ran up there, told him not to let go until I told him, and straightened out my team back to the trail. I told him he could let go and went merrily on my way.

A real good friend and fellow competitor had a problem with those same stones. She fell down and did what you are supposed to do. She hung on for dear life and dragged over those stones. She broke her knee and never ran dogs again. Maybe I made the right choice.

Nanook leading my team after I finally inherited him. We were racing at Sugarloaf Mountain. His sister, Wolfie, was at point.

Nanook became my lead dog after Frank had used him for years. The race I remember him best for was when our club and a snowmobile club joined together and ran across Michigan- well we ended up going from Traverse City to just past Grayling. Each dog team and driver had a snowmobile and driver to go together. We stopped overnight in Kalkaska. We had moose stew which the Kalkaska Snowmobilers served us and we stayed in tents on the clubhouse grounds. I think only the dog drivers stayed in tents. I wonder where the snowmobilers went? Frank and I planned to share a 2 man mountain tent so we split our equipment between the sleds. Frank took a wrong turn and headed south instead of east. I took a wrong turn but it ended up being a nice way to get to Kalkaska. You can imagine what fun I had waiting for my better half to show up. He only went 50 miles out of his way—but he was fast!! Eventually, we got camp set up, we had our dinner and went to bed. All I remember is the moisture dripping down from the top of the tent but we stayed in our tent all night. Some drivers chickened out and went into the clubhouse to get warm.

Nanook and his fellow lead dog, Sox, took all my commands perfectly. When we came to this real big hill, I hooked my snowhook to the snowmobile and let him inch me on down the hill. Nanook and I weren't stupid! When we got to the finish line, my friend Tom Nixon was petting Nanook and found a growth about the size of a grapefruit between his leg and belly. I don't know how I ever missed it in all the work I had done with him and I felt so guilty that to this day I still feel guilty. He was probably the best lead dog we ever had and I treated him like that. Well, anyway we had it taken off and Nanook went along to all our races and he didn't even need to race.

One time when we were at our cabin in Kalkaska, I went to get Nanook out and he spoke to me with his eyes and begged me to end his misery. The next day we took care of that while I held him in my arms. You know that is the way with any pet. An owner needs to be aware of when he is keeping his pet alive just for his benefit. He needs to be aware of when the animal is no longer enjoying life and is suffering every day. That is when the owner needs to be strong enough to do the right thing.

Millie leading my team coming down a hill in Johnson Park in Grand Rapids, Michigan.

Millie was my lead dog while Frank was using Nanook and Boots. She was a short legged, rather small dog and a little chubby if we didn't work hard on it. She and Comet came as a pair of point dogs from Joe Redington in Alaska. Neither one made Frank's team but both of them became lead dogs for me. Millie was a single lead for me. She did not know gee and haw (left and right commands) but I could drive her perfectly with the no command. If she went the wrong way, I just said no and we'd be off on our right trail.

The race I remember most about Millie was one in Kalkaska. Frank and I both were running in the unlimited class. I left the chute before Frank and it wasn't long before Frank passed me. Millie immediately recognized the head driver as the driver of the team that passed us. She just kicked into another gear and we ran down the trail—Frank Hall team followed by Nettie Hall team. We passed all the teams ahead of us. As I passed all these fellow competitors, I waved at them joyously and continued on my way. I had been driving dogs for a while so I knew better than to let my team run faster than they were capable of sustaining for 20 miles but Millie and I were having such a great time that we continued on. Of course, eventually I lost Frank as he disappeared into the horizon. Millie and I settled down to probably nearly a walk! All those teams that I waved at so gaily, now passed me back. Now they were happy but I didn't care. Millie and I had had a great time. When we came in, Millie just rolled in her harness and I ran up and rolled in the snow next to her. We had a great communication so we celebrated a great race together—we probably either took last or near that.

There was a dentist in Ann Arbor who had a fairly good team. He had a couple dogs left that his wife could use but she needed a lead dog. I gave her Millie to use and she taught the wife all about running and racing a sled dog team. Old, experienced lead dogs can do that. It is actually the best way to get into the sport. We did this kind of thing with our older, experienced dogs.

Pinto was a little female we had purchased from Joe Redington. Before he could ship her to us, she stepped into a moose track and somehow this caused her not to be able to lead anymore. We said we wanted her anyway. She never did lead for us but she ran in Frank's thirteen dog team. She was the only female in the team. Frank liked to run all males so this said something by itself!

She was a very quiet little dog. You hardly knew she was around until she came in heat. She wanted to find the boys then and she would!! She would break chains, climb over fences, dig under fences, break fences, or whatever was needed to get to her guys. It took a long time for me to become aware that it really didn't matter which boy she fell in love with—or two at once, the offspring were very good sled dogs.

One time we had two boys who were on Frank's team and were doing just fine. Suddenly they hated each other so much we could not run them on the same team. When Pinto had her pups that time, we realized that they were each the sire of half the litter. We eventually had to sell one of the boys to get the kennel under control.

Queenie was a little girl I trained to lead. We had sold her as a pup and the people brought her back because when she ran in their team, she came in gagging and breathing extremely hard. They said something was wrong with her breathing. Of course, I gave them their money back and ran her with my own dogs. She had no problem. She had been pulling this other team all by herself because she was so enthusiastic and strong even though she could not weigh more than 35 lbs. I put her in lead of my team and taught her what she needed to know. One of the juniors needed a lead dog so I sold him Queenie. He won most his races the next couple years.

Comet was my lead dog at the time Frank bought me a lead dog for Valentine's Day. I think I was running Comet and Millie double lead but I put Darky, the dog he bought for me from a lady racer from New England, in double lead in that Kalkaska race. Comet was a nice lead dog but she didn't like to pass. The results of the race for me would depend on the draw. If I drew 1st (to be the first team on the course), I was in luck. If I drew behind a fast team, it was OK. If I happened to leave the starting line after a slow team, I had a problem. Since I usually couldn't pass, I was only as fast as 2 minutes faster than the team ahead of me. (We leave in 2 minute intervals).

One of the cardinal rules that Frank and I adhered to was that we never tried anything for the first time in a race. A new gangline had to be tried in training. A new sled had to be used before a race. A new lead dog for sure had to be used at home before putting him in lead in a race. However, that is what we did. Darky and Comet were my double lead in an unlimited race that had 35 entries—several of them former world champions. One of the competitors was of course the lady racer from New England from whom we had purchased Darky. Another was Jean Bryar who was a former woman's world champion and my idol.

A couple years earlier, Jean had come to Oscoda, Michigan. It was an honor for our racing association to have her compete there. She was very helpful to all the Michigan or other mid-west mushers. She was analyzing my team (I was racing in a lesser division) and told me out of my seven dogs only three were doing me any good—or did she say there were only three good dogs in the team. Just in watching me pass her by on the trail where she stood, she truly did pick my three best dogs. I was greatly impressed!

This time we were competing in the same class. Frank came in second in that race but with my new lead dog, I took tenth but more than that, I made a better time than my hero, Jean Bryar.

Darky was a very interesting dog. He looked like and was half lab. He was originally trained by George Attla of Alaska. One of the things George did in training was the use of a chain. While I was working with Darky during the summer after his purchase, he drove me absolutely nuts. I could not make him take his turns correctly but I absolutely refused to use a chain—it was completely against all I believed in training the dogs. Finally, in complete frustration, I got a small chain collar and the next time he refused to do as I asked, I tapped him on the nose with the chain. From then on I or whoever was driving him had a chain collar on the sled. We never had to use it, it was just there. Darky was a perfect lead dog just as he was in that first race.

He was so good I never got to run him again until much

later. Frank having the number 1, Hall team had the best of the kennel—Darky was definitely one of the best. When he became older, again a good friend inherited him from us. He ran on a cross country team which ran slower and longer distances. He was loved so much by his new owner that he was his constant companion until Darky passed away.

Darky and Silky lead as a double lead. Darky was training Silky. Earth was at wheel with Jack. This race was a few years after Frank figured him to slow for his team.

We had another Darky. He was a brown hound-like dog. We got him when we went to help set up the International Sled

Dog Association. We actually picked up a truck load of dogs from a man who was getting out of dog racing. Darky was so shy to even us that we had to walk down her chain in order to get her collar to do what we needed to do. When she was harnessed and in the team, he seemed a little less shy but the fear was that if he ever got loose at a race site, we'd never catch him.

I told Frank, "We have got to get rid of that dog. We'll never catch him if he gets out of the team or the kennel!!"

We argued quite a bit about this. Frank was determined to keep the dog. He finally said, "You run him in your training team and see what you think!!"

I did and when I came back, I said, "If you ever decide to not run that dog, I want him in my team!!" He was so smooth and so consistant that one could never cut him from your team.

He eventually got older and couldn't keep up with our teams so we gave him to a beginner who was having trouble with her beautiful, registered, black and white Siberians. They wouldn't run as a team and definitely would not make the turns she wanted them to take.

It was just the ticket for Mary and her Siberians but it was rather humorous to watch her team come down the trail. Her beautiful Siberians led by an old hound. She'd say sweetly to Darky to gee and Darky would take her perfectly to the right or whatever she wanted. She just loved that old hound and we loved watching her enjoy running her team.

I need to tell you about Boots. I guess the first thing I will do is copy what I wrote when she passed away. Following is what I wrote:

BOOT'S MICHIGAN RACING RECORD

Boots was entered in competition a total of 33 times. In these entries she took 16 firsts, 5 seconds, 2 thirds, and 4 fourths. She placed 27 out of the 33 times. The 6 times not placing were the first 4 races while she was getting oriented to being a lead dog and the last two where this last year when she was starting to show her age.

Boots

HISTORY OF BOOTS

Boots developed a paralysis starting in her tail and progressing up her spine. She was at the vets for several days. On the morning of June 27, 1968, the vet said she was in great pain and nothing could be done to stop the paralysis. He recommended she be put to sleep. At 5 p.m. June 27, 1968, Boots was put to sleep at about 10 years. She was brought home and buried on the edge of the woods, next to her training trail. She was put in a pine box and has a marker that says, "Boots."

Walt Barnhart was the first Michigan owner of Boots. He bought Boots in the summer or fall of 1963. She was purchased not as a lead dog but as a team dog. She was obtained from the Bryars in New Hampshire who had brought her down from Alaska. Walt trained her to be a lead dog.

1964—Walt Barnhart driver

Walt had trouble with Boots the first four races of the season, disqualifying in the first two and taking 8th and 5th in the next 2. In the next six races, he took 5 firsts –the only time being beaten was by Art Allen in Holland and part of the reason for this was that Walt couldn't see the markings for the trail and went down the wrong road for quite some ways. The next day in South Bend, he beat Art Allen by a full minute.

1965—Walt Barnart and Art Dingman drivers

Walt ran the first two and last race of the season, winning 2 out of 3 of the races entered—the last being the Michigan Championship Race at Roscommon. He took third in the other. Walt's team got hit by a car while training and it really disturbed Walt to have 6 of his top team killed. Boots was spared and Art Dingman, Walt's second team driver, took over when Walt just didn't have the heart to compete without his team.

Art ran in three races winning 2 out of 3 and taking 2nd in the one race. This Boots did with a supposedly second rate team behind her.

In December of 1965, Walt became unable to drive because of a back problem. Frank Hall purchased Boots around Christmas of that year. She was overweight and had not been trained for some time.

1966—Frank Hall driver—Boots running double lead with Nanook.

Frank ran in 5 races—won 3, took 2nd in one, and 4th in the last. Frank took his team to Laconia, New Hampshire, so Boots ran in the World Derby, coming in 17th in a field of 30 teams.

1967—Nettie Hall driver

Frank had a knee operation so Tom Mathias was given the pick of the kennel to run in Class A competition—Nettie used what was left in Class B competition. Tom sent Boots back after a trial saying she was getting too old—she was getting older.

Nettie ran 5 races in Class B—won 4 of them and took 2nd in the other. She ran two class A races and took a 4th in one and a 2nd in the last race of the season.

1968—Nettie Hall driver

Having won the Class B Championship by winning every race but 1 in 1967, Nettie felt she should try Class A competition. Boots was to be her lead. She didn't plan to take any trophies but hoped to not come in last. She ran 7 races and took 5 trophies—2 seconds. Boots helped to get 3 of those trophies. At the end of the year, her heart wasn't quite in it and she was officially retired at the end of 1968 racing season—to be used only to train other leads, etc.

A story I wrote about   BOOTS

I'll never forget February 25, 1967. I had been alone for three weeks—Frank was out in New England as helper for Tom Mathias. My team had done really good. We had gone undefeated while Frank was gone but it just isn't as much fun alone. This was the last weekend—today was my last race in Class B competition and I wanted very much to do well.

We were in Grand Haven. The Class B trail was 7 miles long. We started in town on main street and went out along Lake Michigan for 3 ½ miles and then were turned around and took the same trail back. There were 14 teams in Class B—at least 4 of them could beat me if my team and theirs went good; any could if we goofed!

Elly Swanson drew No. 1. George Brew drew No. 2 (he was driving 4 untrained German Shepherds—said he'd wait for me to get out of the chute and follow me all the way. I didn't expect him 100 yds. out of the starting line though.) I drew No. 3. By the halfway mark I was leading the pack which meant I had 13 teams to pass head-on on my return trip. The first pass was simple—Elly had a real good lead also. The second sent shivers down my back when I saw them coming—three teams abreast. One was a competitor, the middle one was George, and the third was a team that had been known to fight. I said, "Gee a little" a little hysterically to Boots and she geed-a-little extra and we made a beautiful pass.

We made 'gee-a-little' passes all the way back. There were cars on the road on either side in town and once in awhile, a moving car. One came right toward us. Boot's natural side was left but there really wasn't room on the left, so I said, "Gee!" and we made a beautiful pass on the right.

Once Elly and I were side by side and we met a team head-on on the road. There was barely room for three teams but Boots held the middle and we passed with no problem.

Coming up main street, meeting those thousands of people on either side of the street must have been a trial for poor Boots as she was a shy dog but I encouraged her on and we came up the main street alone—the first ones that day to cross the finish line.

I lost the race that day. Dennis Houghton took 1ˢᵗ, I took second. But I had something that day that no one can ever take away from me. I ran a perfect lead dog—she did no wrong against some of the worst obstacles that could be put on a race course.

Boots was a funny dog. You couldn't pet her like other dogs and tell her she did a good job. I mean you could pet her but you might as well pet a stone. She'd let you. I had developed a technique of unhooking the dogs on finishing the race and going up and just sitting and talking to Boots for a while. A spectator would perhaps think I was nuts but Boot's eyes told me she understood and that day in Grand Haven, she knew she had done a good job—she was very proud!

The next day was a fun race—the last race of the season. I thought I'd try Class A competition. I had the Class B championship sewed up. It didn't matter how I did in this race. I'd like to finish the race but if I took last, it didn't matter too much. Tomorrow Frank would be home and the racing season would be over. I was tired! That day, it was soon out of the chute that I realized something was wrong. Boots looked back at me with a devilish glint in her eyes. She ran so close to the snowbank on the left that my left hand dogs and my sled were finding it hard to find a place to go. When she took off up the 4 foot snow bank, I knew she must be playing a game—she looked back again with that glint in her eye. We came to an intersection and I said, "Straight ahead!" She made a gee across the road and headed for the wrong direction. At the last minute she straightened out, looked back, and laughed at my being so upset! She saw a curve coming ahead and went full speed ahead, dumping me—I held on though. We came up behind teams but she was satisfied to single foot behind—looking back at me with that glint in her eye.

We took second that day. She never did do anything really wrong but she sure had me in a dither when we got back. She laid there and laughed at me!

Those guys think Boots was their lead dog. They said a woman could never drive her because one never had. Boots and I knew that she was my lead dog. All those other races were just getting ready for me!

On second thought, I think that is all I can say about Boots. Forty-three years later, I have nothing to add except I still love that dog!

When we were attending the Iditarod one year, we were visiting Martin Buser's kennel. Frank was talking to all the people who we were sort of leading around for the dog food company who sponsored Martin. They also sponsored us a couple years and we used their excellent dog food for many years. Eagle Products would take a group of their people up to the Iditarod most years and they enjoyed having us join them. Frank absolutely enjoyed talking to them and I did also. I used to carry heaters in my pocket so the people who weren't used to the cold weather would get a warmed up heater from me. They really appreciated it. We'd both tried to explain what was going on so they could better enjoy what they were seeing.

Biko-My Pick of Buser's Kennel

While we were wandering around, petting all Martin's dogs who were going to go on his team the next day or the ones who would stay home, I went to some of the dogs that caught my eye. I fell in love with Biko. She just missed making his team. If one of the dogs had gotten sick that day, Biko would have gone.

After the race was over—a couple weeks later—we called Martin to congratulate him on how he had done. I don't remember if he won that year but he did four times. Frank mentioned how I had fallen in love with Biko. He said I could have her for $1500. Frank said I wanted her. Actually, we both wanted one of Martin's dogs just to say it was one of Martin's dogs. She was an impressive addition to my team and after I had used her as much as I could, I gave her to a young teenager who was just getting started in dogs. She had a wonderful rest of her life.

Ranger was a lead dog we purchased out in Pennsylvania. He was leading an all Siberian team and doing very good even against hound teams. This was after we had been out of dogs for a few years and I had just retired from teaching. I was sort of starting over. Frank had basically retired from racing dogs except for the senior classic in Kalkaska. The best way to get restarted was to buy an experienced lead dog. Ranger was that plus he was a beautiful black and white.

Ranger and Hus became my lead dogs in the final races of my racing. They were not only a really nice looking pair of lead dogs, they were very dependable and fast enough for my slower, smaller team—usually 6. Ranger and Hus are leading the team on the cover of the book. Ranger's daughter, Thunder, was at point and Ranger's son, Tiger, was at wheel.

Carmack was something else. Bob, one of the top dog drivers and breeders in the state, had given this blue-eyed dog to a guy in Jackson. Carmack had so much energy it was hard to control him. He was given the life of Riley in his Jackson home. He had a jeweled collar and lived in their million dollar home.

One day he was left home alone and wasn't too happy about it. He chewed up the whole corner of his home—or his owner's home. Mrs. Wife said that either the dog or she would go. Carmack went to his new home on McCrum Rd.

Carmack, the Dog we could not hold down.

Carmack was so strong and active that I didn't dare drive or train him, I was getting older and wiser. One time when I was training our teams, Carmack jumped a six foot fence in order to be part of the action. Then I decided we should use him. I ran him in a four dog team. On seeing a picture of me running this team with a plume of snow behind because I basically rode the brake all the way, I decided to trade teams with my second team driver. Chuck drove that team to win race after race. I was so proud of him and Carmack.

He was our star lead dog for a couple of years. We bought his litter mate Rev and the two of them worked great together. We were happy with our teams.

Frank with Rev at our dog truck and carrier.Our back numbers were ready to use or return.My microphone is ready for me to use in announcing who knows what.

One morning after having trained for the following race season, I looked around the kennel because I sensed that something was wrong. I saw Carmack lying on the ground motionless. I went screaming out to him and found he was indeed dead. Folks, I never cry. I cried that day for Carmack.

Some of my Young Kennel Helpers or Drivers

After Ranger, I more often trained other people to run our dogs. We got some good Gordon Shorthair crosses who were able to compete against the best but I figured we weren't going

JOE DUKE

JEFF

JAKE

TRAPPER

NELSON

Joe running a team of one our most loved double leads—Trapper and Nelson.

to win if I drove them while dragging the brake. Joe came one day and wanted to run a team. He became my star driver along with his cousin, Shasta.

Shasta running a team in Mackinaw City.

Joe and I had a good six and four dog team. One winter we traveled to Colorado and raced three races out there and stayed to train during the week. It was a tremendous vacation for me. The only reason I could go is because Bob (who was having divorce problems so he and his dogs were kicked out of home) kept his dogs in our exercise area and stayed in our basement. Frank had someone to help him so I took off to have some fun!

Bob wasn't the first one we helped out when he was in a pickle. We had several people who at one time kept their dogs in our kennels and sometimes joined us in our home.

Dave was one of the young people who helped us the

longest. He started cleaning up dogs at about age 12 and worked for us until he moved to the upper peninsula and started making sleds for himself. He had to fight another neighbor boy who wanted the job of cleaning our kennel for himself. Eventually, I asked Dave if he wanted to go up to Kalkaska with us, help with all the stuff we had to do as chairman of that race, and run a team. He thought a second and then jumped at the chance. He ran a 4 dog team and fell in love with racing. He finally ran his girl friend's dogs and competed in the unlimited class. During this time Dave became an important part of Hall's Sleds. We made him an official employee and even furnished health insurance for him. Frank would make the parts, Dave would put them together, I would sand and varnish, and Frank and Dave or I would finish them up.

Dave and Allie working in production in our business

Allie worked for us for years also. She started by running a three dog team for us but eventually got her own dogs. At one time, I had a deal going with her. I paid her to clean our kennel or whatever needed doing and she kept her dogs in our kennel.

The first 5 she could have there for $5.00 a week per dog. I knew she was interested in getting more dogs so to try to keep her from getting too many dogs, I said after the 5 she would have to pay double for the 6th one and double that for the 7th etc. It didn't slow her down and she started owing me a lot of money. I thought that at some point she would wise up but she went merrily on her way. At this time she was also attending Baker college. When she graduated, we had a party to celebrate. Her parents took her, her friends, and us out to dinner. For a gift I gave her a note saying she was paid in full to Hall's Sleds.

One day when Allie was training her team, she hooked up ten dogs in front of the quad. There was a small covering of snow on the ground. When she cut loose, the quad slid sideways and putting on the brake only caused it to go further sideways. She didn't make the kennel opening but pinned me to the fence. It didn't even break my leg. I guess I had enough cushion. I did get to stand there while she unhooked 10 lungeing dogs. She was some panicked. I did have a nice black and blue leg for some time.

At one time, before she went to college, I thought I could maybe hire her on at a lower pay than Dave but as a regular employee. It didn't take me long to realize that the government was charging me too much to make this possible.

Dave's sister, Lainie, and her friend, Deb, wanted to run dogs also. Lainie was doing some work for me. I had a nice truck with a 24 dog carrier so I could carry the dogs for them. I decided I would buy a small travel trailer and pull it to the training sessions and races. I spent all summer preparing the trailer and had it fixed up really fine. Frank was definitely not approving of this plan. He helped me when I asked but he wasn't happy about it

We left for our first training session. We got lost on the way up and I had to turn the truck and trailer around in the dark on a lonely country road. We got it all set up and went to bed. It was super comfortable! During the night, it started to rain pretty heavy. The trailer leaked in the back and things turned just plain miserable. That was one of the times I had to admit Frank was right and I was wrong!

Both girls did run 3 dog teams that season and enjoyed it very much.

Greg came over to look at sleds. His father had passed away tragically and his mother thought this might be something to help him get over his sadness or anger or both. While Frank was chatting with his mother, I took Greg around our trail and kennel. By the time we got back to his mother, I had asked him if he wanted to run team of dogs for me. He was completely thrilled. His mother was eager for anything that would interest Greg. He must have started with a 6 dog team but he was soon running an eight dog team and had set his sister up with a 3 dog team. Mother and the kids went to all the training sessions and races for the next couple years. It made a complete turn around in his life. All my dog drivers went to watch him play soccer at his school.

Junior was a neighborhood friend who never drove a team for me but was my real buddy. I could always count on him to help me out if I had a problem around the kennel. When he married, Carrie became my good friend and helped me put together Frank's book and she will be helping me with mine.

Son Matt ran a team one year in competition. He did quite well. He went up north with Frank when his father ran in a mid-distance race. He and I spent time on the phone as he helped Frank with him up there. Frank didn't stop the snowmobile behind Matt while Matt was on snowmobile sled ahead of him. They were working on marking or grooming the trail. Matt broke his let. That was the sad ending of Matt's sled dog racing.

The year Matt was racing, Rick raced another team for us. He ran one of the fastest three dog teams we ever had. I think he won every three dog race that year. Sarge was his lead. Sarge was a half greyhound and had all the desire of a husky. In one race in Minnesota, Sarge finished the trail which was near the start. He turned and started right on down the trail again. The crowd was ecstatic. Rick couldn't stop the team so a bunch jumped in and helped him stop.

Sarge was half greyhound

Early in our racing, Dave, our neighbor, fell in love with my twin, blue-eyed grey and white malamute type dogs. We sold him a team of dogs and he used our trail to train his team. He and Dean, who was running a 7 dog team for us, went along with me to all the races while Frank was out East running his unlimited team. They both enjoyed partying at the race sites.

One race in Houghton Lake, they had got up with bleary eyes. Dave was doing his dogs and Dean started on mine. We had two pails. One held the chain which we dragged out and secured so we could tie out the dogs to relieve themselves. The other was our 'shit bucket.' Dean was sleepily dumping the droppings, which were a little runny that morning, in the chain bucket. For some reason, it did not seem humorous to me. I was so very angry! This time I wasn't even nice. I let them know that blank blank blankity blank, I didn't think it was funny and they should quite spending all night entertaining themselves, and they needed to be on top of their game at the races!!!

Puppy Keemo and Kayto who grew up to be the beautiful, blue-eyed brothers who Dave couldn't resist.

**When we trained from the kennel, we picketed the
dogs down along the pens so it was just a few steps to
the gangline. It made it a lot easier for me than to bring
them on down a big hill to hook them up.**

Trent Palmer-Vance
2005 Kinross Classic
Kinross, MI

Trent with Colt and Rob in double lead.

After I could no longer run or train our teams, we sold our teams to Dave B. and his son Trent. Dave had been running a second team for our neighbor who lived 15 miles away. We gave him a chance to have his own dogs by selling him the team and allowing him to keep his dogs in our kennel at no expense as long as he would feed, clean up after, and train the team. He also had to transport the dogs to the races. He lived 25 miles from our home. He had some really great dogs of great breeding. Bob and Rob were his lead dogs. There could be none better. In a couple years, Trent took over as driver. When Trent graduated from high school, they had to sell the dogs. This happens so often in families of mushers. Their star driver graduates and the mushing life is over. Often these same drivers go back to mushing when their education is completed.

After they sold their dogs, we had only one dog left. Trapper had been our dog since a puppy. We loved him dearly. One night I guess I didn't latch his kennel good enough or he missed his friends so much, he left in the middle of the night. He's the only dog we ever lost! I still feel frustrated about it. I hope he found himself a new home because he was beautiful and had a wonderful disposition.

Trapper

On Being President or Something on the GLSDA Board

Since I was a good organizer, I often found myself on the board of the Great Lakes Sled Dog Association. Several times I was president. I think I was everything on the board except 1st VP. This position was in charge of getting races and making sure they went OK. One year I had to do the job of both president and 1st VP. What else could I do when my person in charge of that did nothing. Anyone who has had that experience knows how that works.

I enjoyed being president or whatever and going to the board meetings. That way you keep abreast of what is going on and what people are thinking in regard to the issues discussed.

Some said that GLSDA could not survive without me. When I left the racing scene for many years, the association did just fine which proves these people wrong!

The kids lining up for their ribbons.

One of the things I enjoyed most was the kiddie races. We had a junior 2 dog, one mile race and a junior 1 dog race. Anyone could enter this. They could preenter or enter at the time of the race. They could only race on one day—either Saturday or Sunday. We did keep combined times and gave trophies to the first two places. We also gave ribbons each day for that day's race. Sometimes a family would all run the same dogs 2 or 3 times. Sometimes they would run their family pet. Sometimes they ran someone's lead dog. In any case, after the race, I'd call, "Ribbon time, ribbon time."

All the contestants came back and we gave ribbons to the first 10 places and participation races to anyone who ran the race. This kiddie race was a favorite of the crowd. We often ran it while the unlimited were out on the trail. This way the spectators would have something to watch while waiting for the big teams to come in. Some dogs would scoot right down the trail. Some would stop half way to relieve themselves or to go into the crowd and call it a day.

Since I was so organized, I wanted to make sure everything the day of the race would be going like clockwork. The first part of the day on Saturday, I'd walk around with this serious look on my face and make sure that all the workers were doing their work and all the teams were aware of when they would be going to the starting line. If you missed your chute time, you went to the back of the pack which if there were 30 teams in your division, you had a huge penalty.

On Sunday, as soon as I finished racing or my teams finished racing, I started making sure the trophy/ prize money was organized for the end of the race meeting. I made sure someone was ready to speak on needful subjects, the checks were written and put in the order to be presented, and the trophies were displayed in the order in which they were to be presented. My goal was for the meeting to start 15 minutes after the last team came across the finish line. I wanted everyone to be present at the meeting. It is awful hard for a team to wait an hour for presentations when they have miles to drive in sometimes bad weather so they can be to work on Monday morning.

I was most proud of a drivers' meeting before one of the Kalkaska races. I was running the drivers' meeting which I most often did. I didn't trust anyone to keep it moving but myself! Again, it is hard to wait through a drivers' meeting for a couple hours when you need to get things ready for the race on the morrow. Some things have to be covered like the passing rules and time schedules and who the officials are.

I'm receiving my honorary life time member award in ISDRA. Dave Steele, Executive Secretary of ISDRA, and Margaret Harvey, President of GLSDA. Frank and I both received honorary life time member awards in GLSDA

This Kalkaska race was one where there were 25 plus teams in unlimited and a 100 plus teams in all. Many past world champions were in attendance. When it came to introducing the drivers, instead of going around the room and letting them introduce themselves, I went around the room introducing each one. I gave the name and where they were from of every person there. The only mistake I made was I introduced one gal by her maiden name instead of her married name—I quickly corrected myself. I think back now when I have trouble remembering names all the time, how amazing that I could do that. I was so proud of myself!! Please forgive me for my lack of humility!!

It always seems to be hard to get people to be involved in the running of the association. It does take a lot of time sometimes but an active club is a healthy club so one should always think how they can help.

Retiring from Racing in the Middle Years

Teaching became harder for me as I neared retirement. I needed to spend more time on preparation and being rested so I could handle problems in the classroom. It eventually became hard for me to get up in the morning, go to school, come home to train dogs (we often had kennel boys who cleaned up the dogs), help Frank with making sleds (I did most of the sanding and varnishing), feed the dogs, make dinner, and then work on homework until 12 to 2 in the morning. Something had to give!! Racing was it.

One of things we did when we were not going to races on the weekend is we started going to a local church. We both felt comfortable there. We had both been raised in the church. As a youngster, I was always questioning as to why I couldn't dance, go to movies, or have a glass of beer. I couldn't dance and I didn't like beer so that was no problem but I really did enjoy movies. Although I went to church Sunday night and morning, Wednesday night, and any time something was going on in church, I never made a personal commitment to Jesus. I went because I had to go. One night, when Frank and I had started attending church, as I was reading a book by Billy Graham, I decided to take his advice and just give myself to Jesus. As a new Christian, I was again involved in church but it was different now. I wanted to be there instead of having to be there.

One of the things that they talked me into was being on the softball team. I had played softball in elementary school. One time they let me pitch and I walked everybody until they had someone pitch for me. I had pitched for the practice team and did well but being in a real game was different. I pitched in both high school and college and did fine. When they realized I knew something about the game, they got on my case. I soon took over leadership of the team and it wasn't long until we had around 24 girls playing on the team. Some of us weren't too good but we had an awfully fun game. We did become fairly good. I never pitched but rather usually played short stop. I really enjoyed it.

In racing I was drawn to the Junior High and High School kids and the same was true in church. I was soon the leader of these students on their Weds. night meetings.

My Junior High-High School friends in racing. Greg, Jordon,Courtney, and Bill. My favorite dog truck with a dog carrier Frank made from an electrical vehicle. It was a nice little outfit but it could carry 10 dogs-a 6 dog and 4 dog team. Joe and I took this truck to Colorado for 3 weeks of racing.

Frank, me, daughter Laura and her friend. This was taken as we reentered Alaska after visiting the Yukon.

One summer while retired from racing, we decided to take a trip to Alaska. We took the plane to Vancouver, the ship to Skagway, a bus to Dawson City and Fairbanks, a train from there to Denali Park and Anchorage, and a plane back to Michigan. Frank wanted to follow the route of the Gold Rush of around 1848 or something so we took the bus up to Dawson. He had read so many books about it that he really acted as the narrator as we rode. One of the side trips we took was a boat on the Yukon. We were taken past a kennel on the shore to see them feeding their dogs. That made us feel at home! One of the highlights was the tour into Denali Park. We skipped the special where you could take a ride with a dog team. Our old friend and competitor, Lavon Barve came on board in Wasilla and answered questions of our group. We really did enjoy that.

During the racing, teaching, building, and hunting, we always continued our business.
I always helped until I declared Hall's Sleds was no more.

Things were not as exciting as when we were training and racing our teams but we lived a more normal life.

After I retired from teaching, we got back into racing. Again it was hard to get to church on Sundays if we were competitive in the races.

Varnishing the sleds was basically my job.
Summers I'd dog it outside. Winters I'd do it inside—in
our house trailer at first, then in the shop, and finally in
our special varnishing room
Here I am in our old shop

I did a lot of the router work also.
Here I am working on runners getting ready to bend on the long tube.
I am in our new shop.

Hunting

One Thanksgiving, Frank and his cousin and wife decided we should all go hunting. They suited me up nice and warm and put me in a place where I might see/shoot a deer. I sat there and got more cold and more cold. Finally I talked to myself that if per chance I should see a deer, my hands would be so cold I wouldn't be able to pull the trigger and besides if I saw a deer, I would never shoot it in a million years. I'd enjoy looking at it but I would never shoot it. I got up, walked to the car, tried to open the door which I finally did and sat inside. I never went hunting again. The end!!!!

Building our House and Cabin

Before we built our house, we discussed whether we should move north. I checked around at various school districts. At that time, I was teaching and Frank was working in the body shop. I found that if we did move north I would have to take an awful big cut in pay. I convinced Frank that we should stay in Jackson, build a log home, and make believe we lived in snow country. This would allow Frank to come home full time and make life a little easier for us.

Frank built our basement. I just carried mud.
You can see our kennel and cache in the background.

We were living in a house trailer on our land at that time. We had built a basement on which to build the house. We spent one winter vacation cutting down white pine trees growing in a pine planting of 25 years ago that needed thinning. We had to pay 10 cents a foot. We had a tractor that just fit between the trees. Our kennel boy at that time was a strong, husky young man named Ted. Frank was good with the chain saw. We went to work. Frank designed a trailer so long—actually the main hitch was on a long log secured to the rest of the trailer. Frank would choose the trees that were the tallest and straightest. We would load them on the trailer by dragging them and then rolling them on the trailer. We'd drive home with around 6 logs. Then we would unload them by rolling them off.

When we thought we had enough logs, we went back to our racing while letting the logs air out.

When spring vacation came, we began building our house. We had one small book that we used as a reference. We drew up the plans so we would have a small house but open enough so we could entertain a large number of people. Vinnie from Canada was supposed to help us get started but since he was on trapper time, we were 6 logs up when he arrived. He did help us with the windows and doors and we certainly enjoyed his company.

I would peel the logs and Frank would notch them. I became a professional stripper that spring. Pine logs give off a sticky substance and this would stick to my pants and through to my legs. I had to tear them off from my skin until I thought to wear two pairs of pants. One I stood up in the corner and the other was the one next to my skin. It would take me about as long to peel a log as from Frank to notch the two corners so it fit snugly.

We are six logs up. You can see my peeled logs waiting to go up.
You can see all my chips littering the ground.

When we got to the top log (the ridge pole) we decided to have a party. Our little book said we should. It didn't tell us how to do it. So we had a party. We invited people important to us and to our house. That ridge pole just swung in the breeze. It was only held in place by the logs on either end of the house. Someone thought they should walk the ridge pole but fortunately changed their mind.

We thought we were about finished. We had all the logs up to the plate log. We had the support and the purlin up half

**This is in the midst of our party.
The guys actually lifted the ridge pole up manually.
The truck did help us to lift some the logs up where
they belonged.**

way up the roof. The ridge pole was in place and we had the party! We started on the roof. It was then we calculated that we needed 30 logs on either side. They each needed to be peeled and notched in three places-at the plate log, at the purlin, and at the ridge pole. They needed to be perfectly level to support the roof boards. That included that one side needed to be flat! We finally figured that out by taking them all across the road to where a portable saw mill was working and had a little cut off the one side. That would give us a level roof if we notched correctly at the three places.

That took us a lot longer than we had figured but we finally got it done. We bought 4 by 8 foot plywood. The total cost for the flat boards was $400.00. The total cost for our logs was also $400.00. All in all, it was really very cheap but there were tons of sweat spent over the time.

The paint or covering for the logs was a mixture of boiled linseed oil, a bug prohibitive of some sort, and some baby powder to thicken it up a little. We put around 5 coats on both the inside and outside. By this time it was June and I needed to go into the hospital for some kind of surgery. Besides, we had run out of money.

Our completed log home

The next year after the race season, we put in the separations for the rooms, picked up flat stone in the fence rows for the fireplace, and put that in place. We ran out of money.

The next year, the furnace in our house trailer backed up

and we were breathing impure air. One day I went to buy our bedroom furniture and had it delivered to our log house. That night I informed Frank that I was going to sleep in our new

Our friend, Marilyn Clothier, gave us this tooled leather clock.
It was a house warming gift.
On it were each of our teams.
Frank was running Nanook.
I was running Boots
At that time we could identify each of our dogs in both teams

house! There were no toilet facilities hooked up yet but I figured I could run down to the trailer during the night if I needed to do so. Frank was happy to join me. We fixed up the plumbing that year and I suppose then we probably ran out of money again. The neat thing about running out of money was that when we finally finished the house, it was paid in full.

A few years later we bought about 10 acres in the Kalkaska area. We decided to build a log cabin on that property. We had moved our truck camper up there and our neighbors, our

Putting up our vertical log cabin

good friends, Tom, Shirley, and family, lived next door. They had purchased the 10 acres right next to us. They were living in town at a motel while they were working on their land. I convinced Frank that we should let them live in our camper so they could save money and get more work done on their land.

The 5 of them lived in the camper for at least 6 months

until they moved into their partially finished house.

We decided to cut the trees off our land—they were not that big around—and build a vertical log cabin. We immediately decided we didn't need a log roof—remember the 30 logs on each side of the roof! I spent that summer up in the north woods, staying in our camper, and peeling small logs. It seemed like thousands were needed for a vertical log cabin. Frank would come up on the weekend and put the logs in place. It was really a very relaxing summer.

Our completed cabin all ready to accept guests.

We built the cabin so deer hunters and mushers could come in bunches and train on our trails. We had two bedrooms and loft over each. Then there was the sofa and other places you could put folks. We invited everyone to join us over the Christmas holiday. We hadn't put in the plumbing yet but I had a neat little portable toilet that I could empty once a day so all was set to go.

The first truck load came. I helped them settle their dogs in a good place on the land and helped them to move into the cabin. Then I explained the training trails and helped them hook up their dogs to run them. The next truck load came. I helped them settle their dogs in a good place on the land and helped them move into the cabin. Then I explained the training trails and helped them hook up their dogs to run them. Frank spent his time entertaining the first group. I found my port-a-potty full so I needed to empty it and refill the water. Then the next truck load came. I helped them settle their dogs in a good place on the land (it was getting more scarce) and helped them move into the cabin. Then I explained the training trails. The port-a-potty was full again so I needed to take care of that. I helped them hook up their dogs to run them. We needed to run our dogs, so we did that. The port-a-potty was full again and so on and on and on. Everyone had a fantastic time. The trail was beautiful. The days were full of good cheer until 1 AM or so. My guests did most of the cooking and cleaning up.

After we had cleaned up the cabin and got everyone including us on our way home, Frank and I discussed our cabin. I told him that under no circumstances was he to invite anyone to our cabin the next Christmas on penalty of death!! Actually we did invite one new couple to the cabin and we had a very restful Christmas vacation. I didn't even need to take care of a port-a-potty that year!!

Frank and his buddies spent many wonderful hunting seasons up there and we spent many great training times up there. It was a little bit of heaven.

Teaching

From what I've been talking about, you'd think teaching was a small part of my life. I loved teaching and spent many years doing the best I could in the classroom. I taught about 6 years in Grandville, MI. While there, I continued my education by taking extension classes in Grand Rapids, MI. I had taken all my required courses for my degree. I needed to spend the summer on the University of Michigan campus but only needed 8 hours of electives. I received my MA of Education degree.

My parents lived in Florida and I decided to teach there. I taught one year and Frank came down and we decided we should go back to Michigan. We ended up in Jackson.

Carole and I with our husbands, Richard and Frank
This was taken at my retirement party

A couple years after I started teaching, I teamed up with Carole Straayer and we team taught together for about 25 years. I felt Carole was the absolute best reading teacher I'd seen and she thought I was pretty good teaching math. I felt honored to have my kids taught reading and social studies by her while I taught her kids math, English, and science. We got so that we could exchange plans without doing much talking. We'd make plans for the afternoon while the students exchanged places—just with a couple of words or nods.

One year we separated because I wanted to try a new computer teaching program in one of the schools. I studied all summer so I understood the principles and processes of the program. I was abhorred when I realized the other teachers hadn't worked on it at all before the beginning of the school year. I spent a lot of time at the beginning the year getting them all acquainted with it.

One of the reason I was so interested in this program was that my method of teaching math was individualized. I taught each at the point where they were so no good math student was held back by anyone, no one who found it harder to do math was left behind, and each progressed at his own speed. The computer program more or less did this with all the subjects.

The last year I taught, we proposed to the school board that we would share a class, I would teach the students or teachers how to use the computers the school board had put in their rooms and they were just sitting there unused, and Carole would work with the student teachers who sometimes got good critic teachers and sometimes didn't. She was super working with student teachers. The school board figured they couldn't afford that so I decided I needed to retire!!!

Back on the Farm

When I was young, I lived on a small farm near Coopersville, Michigan which is near Grand Rapids. We had 40 acres which is the same that Frank and I owned in Jackson later. My dad rented or share cropped around 200 acres around us. I had three older brothers and one younger sister.

The fact I was the first girl probably influenced my life on the farm quite a bit. I was my father's pet. Things had turned around on the farm since my brothers were my age. They went

Flicka harnessed up to go berry picking

without a lot. I was given the choice of either having a horse or a bike. I got both. That kind of thing bothered my brothers. I was a tomboy. I loved helping my dad so I got to do it a lot. My sister, Gerarda, was stuck in the house helping Ma and I was out in my glory helping Dad. We'd have a contest to see who could milk our cows faster. We'd have another contest to see who could throw the bales of hay higher in the loft. My brothers hated farm work so guess what? I was my dad's favorite!

My sister and I drove my horse Flicka a couple miles to pick strawberries.

I was 10 years younger than my oldest brother and Frank was also 10 years older than me. It made a big difference in how each of us approached money. Money burned a hole in my pocket. If I had cash in my pocket, it was gone. Therefore Frank was the money keeper. Frank kept everything and anything of value because we might need it some day. The two of us made a good couple in that he made me be careful of our money and I urged him to let loose a wee bit. My brother didn't get all the things that I did and when we were younger, we didn't really understand why that was so.

My sister, Gerarda (Gera), and me

I was born with long fingers. My parents figured I'd be the piano player in the family. I took lessons for 5 years and still could not play good enough to play for someone singing. My sister came along and the piece that I was struggling with playing, she could play beautifully by ear. It wasn't long until my parents and I gave up on me. I just loved sitting on the piano bench and sing along with my sister for an hour at a time.

We loved to sing together.
My parents thought we were very good!
My sister was good. She played the organ at church
and elsewhere.

High school was at Coopersville High, but my grade school was 9 years at Lillie school which was the one room country school a quarter of a mile down the road. My youngest brother had some health problems. It was my responsibility to watch out for him during the school day. Although he was a year older than me, we were in the same grade. We had a huge class. There were six of us. My sister was in a class of two. My dad was the superintendent of the little school.

A school picture in 1945.
My sister in the front row. My brother is in the back row. I'm in the second row
I think I'm wearing braids and am very skinny (shock).

Reading was my thing in grade school. I had read every book in our library and they had to get extra books from someplace to help me out. I don't remember much studying except in helping my brother but my grades were pretty good.

Softball was my thing for sports. We had a softball team that went around playing other one roomed schools in the area. Butch was our pitcher. I forget what I played but I was the back-up pitcher. When we practiced at our home school, I would pitch for the other team. One game they decided I should be given a trial as the pitcher. I think I walked around 3 times around when they decided I should give it up.

One day we had a game scheduled and our teacher was home sick. We didn't see why that should stop us since was all had bikes. Our equipment was in the school. No problem!! I crawled through some small window into the furnace room, got our equipment, and we were on our way. We biked to Lamont, drove back and forth over the signal at the gas station, and played our game. I don't remember if we won the game.

I do remember that I was in trouble the next day. I was kicked out of school for at least a day. I can believe that the teacher must have been frustrated when I rode my bike around the school while I was suspended. I'm sure my dad heard about it and dealt with it in some way.

When I went to high school it was a big change for me. I enjoyed the school work and did a real good job on it but I had a hard time with having so many classmates. I did enjoy Phys. Ed. and again pitched for their team. When I went to college, I pitched for their team and did a good job. When I played later, I could never pitch again. I just loved to play wherever they needed me.

All through high school I still was the tomboy and helped around the farm. I'd milk the cows before getting on the bus. When I got home, I'd do the evening chores which included milking the cows. When it came time to decide on a college, I realized I could not go to college during the week and then spend the weekend being the farmer. I also had no real desire to go to college but I did want to teach which meant I had to go to college.

My brother had gone to Hope College in Holland, Michigan but I knew that would not work for me. Hope College

Frank and I reliving our farm days while doing our garden.
Frank driving tractor. I'm running the cultivator.
We actually enjoyed doing this kind of thing.

had a sister college in Pella, Iowa. The neat thing about this was that I could go for just 2 years and be eligible to teach—in a Christian school. Being in Pella would mean I couldn't come home every weekend.

After being in college a year, I realized two things. First, college wasn't all that bad, as a matter of fact, I loved it. Second, I really needed four years of college to be prepared to teach. I transferred to the four year plan.

My Final Years

Frank passed away on Sept 14, 2007. Not long after that I realized I could not go on with the sled business alone. I also knew that no one would make the sleds up to Frank's perfection. Therefore, I declared Hall's Sleds was no more. I had an auction and sold almost everything I had left after selling much of Frank's things for a token to his many friends. I kept some things that were precious to me.

Now I live in a retirement type home. I wonder what my life would have been like if I'd never met my true love, Frank.

Retired!!